★ ★ ★ ★ ★

THE NEED OF OUR
NATION

★ ★ ★ ★ ★

SCOTT PAULEY

A resource from…

First Edition » Copyright © March, 2021 by Scott Pauley

All Scripture quotations are taken from the King James Version.

First published in 2021 by Enjoying the Journey in partnership with Faithworks Media. Faithworks Media exists to provides high-quality church print resources and evangelistic material which *"adorn the doctrine of God our Saviour in all things."*

Cover design and layout by Stephen Troell
Editing, proofreading, and assistance by Greg Dowdy, Tammy Jones, Lauren Pauley, and Monroe Roark.

ISBN 978-0-9974816-8-6
Printed in the United States of America

"For the Furtherance of the Gospel" » **faithworks**media.com

During the time that Jesus lived on this earth, Rome had the greatest expansion in its history. While a pagan government was broadening its reach and wicked men were in power, our great God was doing His most wonderful work in this world! Caesar is gone, but the church of Jesus Christ is still advancing.

God's Word has the answer to the dilemmas of every age. *"For the LORD is good; his mercy is everlasting; and his truth endureth to all generations"* (Psalm 100:5). Truth transcends all language, time, and cultural bounds. In the following Bible meditations, found throughout the Old and New Testaments, the Holy Spirit speaks to the deepest needs of men and nations. There are no social, moral, economic or political solutions to a spiritual problem. The hope of a nation is in what God is able to do, and the need of a nation is for people who know how to pray.

· INTRODUCTION ·

SHAKING FOUNDATIONS

Though I have not personally experienced an earthquake, I have talked to people who have, and they say it is one of the most disconcerting experiences because the very thing you think is most stable—the ground under your feet—is giving way. Everything is shaking. Everything is uncertain.

THE NEED OF OUR NATION

Have you ever felt that way—like the world is spinning out of control, with the wicked winning, and you do not know exactly what to do next?

Several years ago, we were building our house in West Virginia during a season when we saw an unbelievable amount of rain. I remember the builder said, "Scott, we are having a difficult time just getting your footers poured and getting the foundation where it needs to be. We've been pumping water out so we can try to pour the concrete." "Let's just slow down," I said. "Let the water subside and the weather pass." I knew I wanted a solid foundation.

Foundations are very important. Look at a house that has been built on a poor foundation. It doesn't matter how beautiful the house looks on the outside if the foundation is crumbling. Over time, cracks appear. It is more than just settling; it is a subtle shift that compromises the integrity of the entire structure.

We are seeing this in our world today—a shifting in families, churches, and lives. It seems, at times, that the foundations of our society: godliness, decency, and family, are being destroyed. Occasionally, God's people can feel absolutely overwhelmed to a point of desperation, not only by what we see, but also by what we hear. We look at current events and get the sense that our nation is coming apart at the seams. The foundations are certainly shaking.

THE NEED OF OUR NATION

In Psalm 11, we find a nation in turmoil. David had been anointed as the next king, but Saul, the current king of Israel, was trying desperately to kill him. All of his friends said, "David, get out of there. Run for your life. It's the only hope you have."

In that setting, God was teaching David to wait on the Lord and to live by faith. That is the context of one of the greatest psalms in all of Scripture. It is the psalm of both a nation and a man in turmoil, wondering what can be done.

Listen to the Holy Spirit-inspired words, beginning with the first three verses: *"In the Lord put I my trust: how say ye to my soul, Flee as a bird to your mountain? For, lo, the wicked bend their bow, they make ready their arrow upon the string, that they may privily shoot at the upright in heart. If the foundations be destroyed, what can the righteous do?"*

This question leads us back to the God of all answers. Immediately after the question posed in verse 3, we read these words in verse 4: *"The Lord is in his holy temple, the Lord's throne is in heaven: his eyes behold, his eyelids try, the children of men."*

Instead of looking down in frustration and discouragement, we are told to look up in faith. Instead of concentrating on what we think is going on, we are instructed to look at the spiritual reality: *"The Lord is in his holy temple."*

I want to remind you that God is seated on the throne of the universe, and that the foundations in Heaven are not shaking at all. According to 1 Corinthians 3:11, *"For other foundation can no man lay than that is laid, which is Jesus Christ."*

It is essential to get our eyes off this world and on the only One Who never changes. Even if the foundations of this world crumble, our foundation is never destroyed because it is in Heaven.

In a changing world, the foundation of our lives is the unchanging God. He says, *"For I am the LORD, I change not…"* (Malachi 3:6).

Our foundation is not some political cause, nor is it some person. David was, without a doubt, disillusioned with King Saul and wondered what would become of him amid the chaos. But David's faith was not in a man; it was in God. He was reminded by the Holy Spirit that the Lord was exactly where He had always been—on His throne. That should encourage us today as well.

The Bible says in 2 Timothy 2:19, *"Nevertheless the foundation of God standeth sure, having this seal, The Lord knoweth them that are his. And, let every one that nameth the name of Christ depart from iniquity."* There may be a great deal that we do not know about the future, but God knows those who belong to Him. He rules in Heaven and holds His children on earth in the palm of His hand (John 10:28-29).

We are told in Revelation 21:14, *"And the wall of the city had twelve foundations, and in them the names of the twelve apostles of the Lamb."* That is the city where we will live someday. It is a reminder that whatever the Lord does will last forever (Ecclesiastes 3:14). It is eternal. It cannot be shaken.

The answer to the question asked in Psalm 11, verse 3 is actually this: the foundation is not being destroyed. The real question is, "If our foundation is in God, why are we trembling?" If you ever begin to wonder, as a child of God, what to do in the midst of unrighteousness, this psalm gives you direction.

· PSALMS 11-12 ·
WHAT CAN WE DO?

Psalm 11 and 12 are twin psalms. Taken together, they answer the pressing question that is on everyone's minds: What can we do? While there are many things we cannot change, there are specific things God teaches that we all can do.

What can we do? We can trust.

That is what David wrote in the first verse of Psalm 11, *"In the LORD put I my trust."* This is not just a Christian cliché. "Trust the Lord" is not a flippant statement to make when someone you know is going through difficulties. The Lord is our Anchor, and when the way is unclear and the waters are rough, only the Lord can give stability (Hebrews 6:17-20).

Anything that does not begin in faith will end in failure. Trust that God has you exactly where you are supposed to be. He is working even in circumstances that are less than desirable. And you can trust that God is always where He is supposed to be. Psalm 11:4-6 says:

> *The Lord is in his holy temple, the Lord's throne is in heaven: his eyes behold, his eyelids try, the children of men. The Lord trieth the righteous: but the wicked and him that loveth violence his soul hateth. Upon the wicked he shall rain snares, fire and brimstone, and an horrible tempest: this shall be the portion of their cup.*

How sad that so many believers live like unbelievers! The greatest temptation is not the enemy you see, but the temptation to live by sight and not by faith. The Christian life, from beginning to end, is a faith life (Hebrews 10:38, 11:1).

David's toughest test was not Saul. It was the urge to listen to everyone around him instead of listening to God. David had to trust that God had him exactly where he was supposed to be even when everyone else told him to flee. When he was tempted to take his life in his own hands, he had to remember that his life was in God's hands, and that is infinitely better.

There are moments when the spiritual attack comes, and the arrows are flying, that we want out. Everyone wants to escape at times, even the most spiritual person. David was no different. Read what he wrote in Psalm 55:3-8:

*Because of the voice of the enemy, because of the
oppression of the wicked: for they cast iniquity upon
me, and in wrath they hate me. My heart is sore
pained within me: and the terrors of death are fallen
upon me. Fearfulness and trembling are come upon
me, and horror hath overwhelmed me. And I said,
Oh that I had wings like a dove! for then would I fly
away, and be at rest. Lo, then would I wander far off,
and remain in the wilderness. Selah. I would hasten
my escape from the windy storm and tempest.*

Perhaps you feel like that today, wishing you could *"fly away"*
from your circumstances. But, be reminded that escape is not
the answer. Your circumstances will chase after you. You will
find new difficulties when you get where you think you want
to be. Your *"escape"* is this: the Lord is still your foundation.

Verse 22 of Psalm 55 concludes, *"Cast thy burden upon
the Lord, and he shall sustain thee: he shall never suffer the
righteous to be moved."*

Escape is not the answer. The only rest and the only victory
is found in trust. *"For whatsoever is born of God overcometh
the world: and this is the victory that overcometh the world,
even our faith"* (1 John 5:4).

The victory is not after the battle ends or when the
circumstances change. The victory is *in* the battle. Remember
that David had been taunted by Goliath, and, in the midst
of that battle, God gave victory. Afterward, when he was

persecuted by Saul, he found victory and rest during that difficulty as well. Even though it felt like the foundations were shaking, as a righteous man, he knew that he could always trust in a God who does everything well.

When we get our eyes back on the Lord, we realize that He has had His eyes on us all along. Look to Jesus today, even in the midst of your turmoil. Do not be dismayed by all of the evil things going on around you. Do not think the devil is winning. One of my favorite songs expresses it well:

> Turn your eyes upon Jesus,
> Look full in His wonderful face,
> And the things of earth will grow strangely dim,
> In the light of His glory and grace.

We look at current events and get the sense that our nation is coming apart at the seams. The foundations are shaking. What are we to do? The need of our nation is the need of every one of our lives—we must *"Have faith in God"* (Mark 11:22).

If you have never trusted Christ as your personal Savior, this is where we all must begin: *"Believe on the Lord Jesus Christ, and thou shalt be saved"* (Acts 16:31). Romans 10: 8-9 says: *"The word is nigh thee, even in thy mouth, and in thy heart: that is, the word of faith, which we preach; That if thou shalt confess with thy mouth the Lord Jesus, and shalt believe in thine heart that God hath raised him from the dead, thou shalt be saved."* Call on the Lord now in simple faith and He will keep His Word.

If you know the Lord Jesus in a personal way, this is the time to exercise your faith in His sufficiency. The same God who is able to save from hell is able to help us in our present circumstance. Say with David, *"In the Lord put I my trust."*

What can we do? We can stay right with God.

Our faith must be lived out in every area of life (James 2:17-18). Trusting the Lord is expressed by obeying Him. After teaching us to believe God, Psalm 11 concludes in verse 7 with, *"For the righteous Lord loveth righteousness; his countenance doth behold the upright."* Our Lord is always righteous, and He wants His people to stay right with Him.

The entire psalm focuses on the righteous and what they can do. How easy it is in an unrighteous world with all that surrounds us to miss the unrighteousness that creeps into our own hearts. Is it possible that, while talking about the need of our nation, we are neglecting the need of our own soul?

Someone asked, "Doesn't all of this wickedness everywhere trouble you?" Absolutely! It vexes me, and it grieves the Spirit of the living God within me. But I am most concerned about the darkness that creeps into my own life. When was the last time you were vexed over your own sin?

We must ask God to help us love what He loves and hate what He hates (Psalm 45:7; Hebrews 1:9). My greatest enemy is not the world. It is the man I see in the mirror every morning. The hardest thing for me to do is to keep myself right with God. Refuse to let the foundations of your own soul be destroyed. Choose to build a life of holiness and obedience.

What can we do? We can pray.

Psalm 11 and Psalm 12 are both very brief and each were written by David. Though they were written at different times in his life, the theme begun in Psalm 11 seems to continue naturally into the next psalm. God's truth will help us at every stage of life. It is a reminder that His way is perfect as we fight every battle and face every burden.

Psalm 12 is a prayer which begins this way in verses 1-5:

> *Help, Lord; for the godly man ceaseth; for the faithful fail from among the children of men. They speak vanity every one with his neighbour: with flattering lips and with a double heart do they speak. The Lord shall cut off all flattering lips, and the tongue that speaketh proud things: Who have said, With our tongue will we prevail; our lips are our own: who is lord over us? For the oppression of the poor, for the sighing of the needy, now will I arise, saith the Lord; I will set him in safety from him that puffeth at him.*

We love to grumble and to complain about how bad things are. Perhaps we should turn our complaining into confession and intercession! Let your conversation become communion with the One person who can do something about the situation.

The contrast in these verses is that the wicked do one thing with their lips while the righteous do something else. Wicked people speak empty words and flatter. God's people are to pray. We must do more than merely fuss at the darkness.

For whom should we pray? This passage suggests four specific types of people:

- We should pray for godly people not to cease (verse 1).
- We should pray for the faithful not to fail (verse 1).
- We should pray for the poor to be protected (verse 5).
- We should pray for the needy to have God's provision (verse 5).

I love the opening words of Psalm 12: *"Help, Lord."* When you cannot do anything else and the foundations seem to be shaking all around you, you can always pray. When you don't know what to pray, you can pray this: *"Help, Lord."* God will answer this simple prayer (Isaiah 41:10).

What can we do? We can meditate.

In the closing verses of Psalm 12, David now encourages us to meditate. First, we call out to the Lord and then we listen to Him. Talk to God and let Him talk to you!

Notice how Psalm 12 ends in verses 6-8: *"The words of the Lord are pure words: as silver tried in a furnace of earth, purified seven times. Thou shalt keep them, O Lord, thou shalt preserve them from this generation for ever. The wicked walk on every side, when the vilest men are exalted."*

Our world is full of wickedness and vile people. None of this can change God and God's Word. *"For ever, O Lord, thy word is settled in heaven. Thy faithfulness is unto all generations: thou hast established the earth, and it abideth"* (Psalm 119:89-90). The world must drive us to the Word.

This is a beautiful picture of the daily fellowship we can have with God even on the most difficult days. Fix your mind on what can never be destroyed, which is the eternal Word of God.

The words of the wicked are lies, as this passage states, but the Lord's words are always true. His word is pure in an impure world. It is preserved in a decaying world, and it will preserve you.

God's Word says, *"Thou wilt keep him in perfect peace, whose mind is stayed on thee: because he trusteth in thee"* (Isaiah 26:3). *"Great peace have they which love thy law: and nothing shall offend them"* (Psalm 119:165).

It has been suggested that the setting of Psalm 12 is one in which all the people and priests who aided David in Nob had been slain by Saul (1 Samuel 22). Everything familiar to him was disappearing, and David thought he might be next. So what did he do? He decided that he would go back and meditate on the words of the Lord. God's Word will give you peace like nothing else can.

THE NEED OF OUR NATION

General Robert E. Lee was a man who knew something about conflict. His favorite hymn was "How Firm A Foundation." One day, the great theologian, Dr. Charles Hodge, was reading the stanzas of that great song to a group of seminary students and was so overcome with emotion that he could not even articulate the last words. I love this particular portion of the song:

> How firm a foundation, ye saints of the Lord,
> Is laid for your faith in his excellent word!

If you think everything is shaking around you, and perhaps even you are a bit shaken today, just stop and spend time meditating on the unchanging truth of the Word of God. Remember, for the follower of Jesus Christ, the foundation is never destroyed. Our foundation is Christ Himself, and our God is never moved.

What can you do? You can trust the Lord. You can stay right with God. You can pray. You can meditate on the truth. The foundation is sure.

Keep close to the Lord, and keep your eyes on His righteousness in the midst of an unrighteous world. He will help you and use you to influence those around you in this needy nation.

A PATRIOT'S PRAYER

What is the greatest need of our nation? After all that we have seen take place in our nation in recent history, it may seem hard to narrow it down to one "greatest" need. Is this need political? Do we need a better education system? Would any of the topics of social reform, equality, or economic stability be considered our greatest need?

The greatest need of our nation is divine intervention.

Psalm 85 was written by a man with a burden for his own people. There is a difference between patriotism and spirituality. A man may be a patriot, but be full of flesh and not the Spirit. However, a Spirit-filled man will always love his country and desire that his *"kinsmen"* come to God. We can make this Spirit-inspired, patriot's prayer our own.

> *Lord, thou hast been favourable unto thy land: thou hast brought back the captivity of Jacob. Thou hast forgiven the iniquity of thy people, thou hast covered all their sin. Selah. Thou hast taken away all thy wrath: thou hast turned thyself from the fierceness of thine anger. Turn us, O God of our salvation, and cause thine anger toward us to cease. Wilt thou be angry with us for ever? wilt thou*

*draw out thine anger to all generations? Wilt thou
not revive us again: that thy people may rejoice
in thee? Shew us thy mercy, O Lord, and grant us
thy salvation. I will hear what God the Lord will
speak: for he will speak peace unto his people, and
to his saints: but let them not turn again to folly.
Surely his salvation is nigh them that fear him; that
glory may dwell in our land. Mercy and truth are
met together; righteousness and peace have kissed
each other. Truth shall spring out of the earth; and
righteousness shall look down from heaven. Yea,
the Lord shall give that which is good; and our
land shall yield her increase. Righteousness shall go
before him; and shall set us in the way of his steps.*

We need God to move and to work. This is our *greatest* need.

There must be a spiritual awakening in our land that only
the Lord can send, and it will only happen when His people
are truly seeking Him. That is why it is so important to
emphasize prayer in these critical days, because it brings us
into the presence of God.

Our need is not prayer; our need is the God to whom we are
praying. It is not about some religious ritual we perform; it is
about the One who hears and answers.

The context of Psalm 85 is not any modern nation. It is
historical Israel, God's chosen people. But the need of that

nation is the same need of every nation: every nation needs God to work.

Our nation and Israel are not the same, but they have the **same problem**: sin and rebellion toward God. It is possible that this Psalm was written after the Jews returned home from the Babylonian captivity. There are three words used in the Psalm that reminds us of why they were in captivity. The writer speaks of *"iniquity," "sin,"* and *"folly"* (vs. 2, 8). Ultimately, Israel's problem was a sin problem. Captivity was how God chastened His people for her sin and turned her heart back to Him. Our own beloved nation has a sin problem. Solomon reminds us that *"sin is a reproach to any people"* (Proverbs 14:34).

Our nation and Israel also have the **same need**, a spiritual awakening. The need is not political revolution, social reform, or economic recovery. It is always spiritual. The prayer of Psalm 85:4 is *"turn us."* Another Psalmist at a different time in Israel's history prayed, *"Turn us again, O LORD God of hosts, cause thy face to shine; and we shall be saved"* (Psalms 80:19). The weeping prophet also prayed in Jeremiah 31:18, *"turn thou me, and I shall be turned."* This is the need of every nation in every generation.

Repentance is always part of the formula for national healing. God promised Israel in 2 Chronicles 7:14, *"If my people, which are called by my name, shall humble themselves, and pray, and seek my face, and turn from their wicked ways;*

then will I hear from heaven, and will forgive their sin, and will heal their land." While it is obvious that our nation needs to be turned to the Lord collectively, it is also critical to understand that we, as individuals, need to be turned to the Lord. This must start in my heart. This must start in your heart. We need God to work and to turn our hearts back to Himself. That is the only hope of any nation.

Our nation and Israel are desperate for the **same person**, someone who knows how to pray. Have you ever considered who the most powerful or influential person is in a nation? The names of many political leaders may immediately come to mind, but the most influential person in any country is the one who knows how to intercede. It doesn't matter who is the best orator or political leader. What matters is who knows how to pray—to enter into the throne room of God on behalf of their own people.

Prayer is the greatest work. It is a humble work, because it brings us low and reminds us how weak we are. It is a holy work because it brings us into the presence of God, and it is the most helpful work because it sends us out differently than we came. While we should labor for righteous causes, vote, and participate in the leadership of our nation, we cannot neglect the most important work—prayer. It was S.D. Gordon who said, "You can do more than pray after you have prayed, but you cannot do more than pray until you have prayed."

THE NEED OF OUR NATION

When was the last time you prayed specifically for your nation? When you did pray, for what did you ask? Were there definite requests for which you prayed? Did you pray in the will of God and expect Him to answer? Or was your prayer with a spirit of aggravation and annoyance with current events? Pray in faith and not out of frustration.

In Scripture, men who had faith and a high view of the greatness of God, prayed for divine intervention in their nation. Moses prayed with brokenness for Israel in the Old Testament (Exodus 32:31-32). He repeatedly interceded for his nation. In the New Testament, Paul prayed for the Jews, his own kinsmen, that they might be saved (Romans 9:1-5). These were men who understood that the greatest need of the nation is always spiritual, and the greatest work a person can do is pray for a spiritual awakening.

Often, when praying for our nation, we pray for peripheral problems or secondary needs. But when a spiritual awakening comes, a great deal of the problems with which we are dealing are remedied. As the gospel breaks through, and the Spirit of God has liberty to move and to work in our nation, much of what we are crusading against at this moment is going to be corrected.

How do we pray for our nation? Pray the prayer of Psalm 85. This prayer begins with the word *"Lord."* It is a direct address to God from someone who loved his country and wanted God to move and to work. In the opening of his prayer he begins with the goodness of God. Rather than creating your own prayer list, use God's Word as your pattern.

Pray with gratitude.

When you begin to pray for your nation, always begin with thanksgiving. This is a foundational principle of prayer throughout Scripture. We read, *"Continue in prayer, and watch in the same with thanksgiving"* (Colossians 4:2). And in relationship to our prayers for others, *"Cease not to give thanks for you, making mention of you in my prayers"* (Ephesians 1:16).

The first three verses of Psalm 85 remind us of past blessings. The phrase *"thou hast"* is used six times to recall what God had already done. Before you ask Him to do anything, remember to thank Him and give Him the glory for past blessings.

In our own beloved country, we have so much for which to be thankful. What a heritage we have been given! Think about the liberty we enjoy and the price that has been paid for it. We should give God glory for every blessing.

As you offer praise, your faith grows. When you are reminded of God's faithfulness, it will increase your faith to pray and believe Him for much more. The same God who answered prayer in the past, and worked in previous generations, is at work today.

The Bible says in Isaiah 59:1, *"Behold, the Lord's hand is not shortened, that it cannot save; neither his ear heavy, that it cannot hear."* God is looking for people who will believe

Him, and He is listening for people who will call out to Him. Sincere praise is a statement of faith in God and a key to effective prayer.

Pray that God will turn our hearts back to Him.

The psalmist began his petition in verse 4 by saying, *"Turn us, O God of our salvation."*

We waste too much time and energy trying to get people to change when that work is reserved solely for the Holy Spirit. He is the One who must do the work in the hearts of people. Only He can turn the heart of a person, and bring the prodigal to Himself. An all-wise God knows what it will take to get our attention.

This Psalm teaches how God deals with us as sinners. First, God works in our heart to *"turn us"* to Himself. Paul said, *"For it is God which worketh in you both to will and to do of his good pleasure"* (Philippians 2:13). God is always the first cause. One of my favorite Bible teachers, Dr. Frank Sells, loved to quote, "God is always previous." Then, after God convicts our heart, we respond to Him in repentance. When we turn from our sin, God turns from His own anger (verses 3-4).

Our nation is in desperate need for God to turn us back to Himself. We must pray that God would work in the hearts of individuals, families, and communities and cause us all to turn back to Him.

Pray for spiritual revival.

When we ask God to bless our country, for what are we asking? When we pray for the blessing of God, we are praying for God's presence. It is our only hope. *"Wilt thou not revive us again: that thy people may rejoice in thee?"* (Verse 6)

The divine order in verse 6 starts with us being revived. We often desire the last part of the verse without experiencing the first part. We want the rejoicing but bypass the reviving. We desire the product without the process. True rejoicing only comes when God is at work in our heart and we are in fellowship with Him.

Very often our prayers for revival are really just prayers for relief. Instead of praying, "Lord, change anything that needs to be changed," we pray that everything will stay the same—that our children and grandchildren will have the same country. That is not the right motivation for this kind of prayer. When real revival comes, it changes the status quo. In fact, God changes everything, beginning with us. We must pray with a repentant heart.

Pray that we might see and hear God.

We live such distracted lives. In our busy, fast-paced schedules, we generally do not make time to listen to God's voice. When there are a few moments of time, we waste them on media and other lesser things. How can we expect a spiritual awakening if we rarely make time to quiet our soul before God? The requests in verses 7-8 are clear: *"Shew us thy mercy, O Lord, and grant us thy salvation. I will hear what God the Lord will speak..."*

The psalmist desired to see God's mercy and to hear His voice. Our spiritual eyes and ears must be opened (Revelation 3:18-20). Imagine the difference it would make in our lives if we spent time every day reading God's Word and praying! What if we started every day listening for God's voice before we heard any other person's voice? What if we closed every day, with an open Bible and an open heart, so that the last voice we heard for the day was God's? Our spiritual vision and hearing must be in tune with God, looking for His hand and listening for His voice.

Each generation must come to know God for itself. In the second half of his prayer, the psalmist concentrates on lasting change. Real revival will produce more than reformation; it will produce transformation. The goal is not merely a religious event or emotional experience, but an awakening that brings us to the knowledge of the truth and a fresh encounter with God.

Pray that we would not turn again from God.

The prayer of verse 8 is, *"I will hear what God the Lord will speak: for he will speak peace unto his people, and to his saints: but let them not turn again to folly."* Remember that in verse 4 his prayer was, *"Turn us, O God..."* Now he prays, *"let them not turn again to folly."*

One of the greatest dangers is after the Lord turns us to Himself, we go right back to our sin. The Bible says in 2 Peter 2:22, *"The dog is turned to his own vomit again; and the sow that was washed to her wallowing in the mire."* This graphic imagery is a picture of sinners going back to their sin.

We must pray that God would deliver us, as a nation and as individuals, from the wickedness that is so prevalent in our land today. This is not just for the short term. We do not seek a temporary change, but instead, desire a true and lasting work of God and grace in our country.

Pray that God would increase those who fear Him.

The psalmist declares in verse 9, *"Surely his salvation is nigh them that fear him; that glory may dwell in our land."*

Glory dwells in the land when it is filled with people who fear God. One of the most important characteristics missing in our nation today is the fear of God. The third chapter of Romans explains the reason why people live in such wickedness and debauchery. It is because *"there is no fear of God before their eyes"* (Romans 3:18).

We pray for glory, but glory is actually a byproduct. Glory rests on those who fear the Lord. We should pray that God will be so lifted up by people who fear Him that His name will be glorified.

Pray for a spiritual stirring in those you love. Families and local churches are the fabric from which this nation is made.

When families and churches are spiritually strong, the nation can be reached. It is easy to become overwhelmed by the magnitude of the need of an entire nation. Therefore, we must start right where we are—in our own home and in our church.

Pray that Christ would be lifted up.

Did you see the Lord Jesus Christ in Psalm 85? Hundreds of years before the Messiah came, these words were written in verses 10-11: *"Mercy and truth are met together; righteousness and peace have kissed each other. Truth shall spring out of the earth; and righteousness shall look down from heaven."*

You may not see His name there, but this passage is a description of Christ. Only in Jesus does heaven touch earth. Mercy and truth met together in the person of Jesus Christ. Righteousness and peace kissed each other at Calvary, where a righteous God and the sacrifice for our salvation met together. Praise the name of Jesus! He is the One our land desperately needs.

We know that someday every knee will bow to Christ and every tongue will confess that He is Lord (Philippians 2:10), but we should be praying for a gospel advance in our nation right now. Pray and ask the Lord how you can be a part of furthering the message of Christ to others. Jesus said in John 12:32, *"And I, if I be lifted up from the earth, will draw all men unto me."* Whenever and wherever Christ is lifted up, the work of God moves forward.

Pray in faith that God would provide everything we need.

This is the prayer that is offered in verse 12: *"Yea, the Lord shall give that which is good; and our land shall yield her increase."* This is a statement of faith. Prayer, by its very nature, is the believer's declaration of dependence on God.

The verse starts with the positive word *"yea."* God's Word also reminds us in 2 Corinthians 1:20, *"For all the promises of God in him are yea, and in him Amen, unto the glory of God by us."* Even though there is much wickedness and negativity in our land, God's people can place their hope in Him, resting in the One who can provide everything they need. Instead of being overcome with the evil around us, we must constantly fix our attention on the goodness of God (Romans 12:21).

Pray that God would guide us in the right way.

Verse 13 says, *"Righteousness shall go before him; and shall set us in the way of his steps."* God's way is always the right way. I remember as a boy following my grandpa through the snow, trying to keep up with his giant footsteps. That is exactly the picture here, that we would follow the wonderful steps of our God.

Many years ago, Charles Sheldon wrote the classic book *In His Steps.* He addressed the idea of what would happen if an entire community answered the question, "What would Jesus do?" Many people have talked about it over the years, but the truth is that this only happens when revival comes. People only consider God in that way when there is a spiritual awakening. Are we ready for God to show us His way?

Pray for yourself.

It is important to notice that throughout Psalm 85, the psalmist included himself. Too many of our prayers are in the third person when they need to be in the first person. It is easy for us to pray, "Lord, revive them." Here, in verse 6, the psalmist asked God to *"revive us."* He included himself.

The Bible says in Psalm 138:7, *"Though I walk in the midst of trouble, thou wilt revive me."* This is where it gets personal. National answers come through personal prayers. National awakenings come through individual revival. It must begin in my heart and it must begin in your heart.

One of the greatest revivals in history, the New Hebrides revival, began when two women and a handful of men got thoroughly right with God and then began to pray for their nation. God sent a great spiritual awakening in response to their prayers. Do you believe that God can do that again? The eternal God identified Himself as *"Jesus Christ the same yesterday, and to day, and for ever"* (Hebrews 13:8). The same God Who sent a spiritual awakening to other generations is still able, right now, to send an awakening that could bring a wayward nation back to Him!

OUR FIRST WORK

Scripture consistently reminds us that the greatest need of every nation is always spiritual. When the spiritual aspect of life is what God wants it to be, every other area of life will be blessed. This is the principle of Matthew 6:33, *"But seek ye first the kingdom of God, and his righteousness; and all these things shall be added unto you."* What, then, is the first call to action for God's people in relationship to our nation?

The first work must be our prayer work. Oswald Chambers said, "Prayer does not fit us for the greater works; prayer *is* the greater work." That is the message we find in 1 Timothy 2:1-4:

> *I exhort therefore, that, first of all, supplications, prayers, intercessions, and giving of thanks, be made for all men; For kings, and for all that are in authority; that we may lead a quiet and peaceable life in all godliness and honesty. For this is good and acceptable in the sight of God our Saviour; Who will have all men to be saved, and to come unto the knowledge of the truth.*

Perhaps you have heard the expression, "First things first." God's priority is revealed by these words: *"first of all."* The first and greatest work is not done in public, but in private. It is the work that is first toward God, not men. If we desire to see a great move of God in our land, then we must move nearer to Him ourselves, and the only way we can move forward is on our knees. D.L. Moody observed, "Every great movement of God can be traced to a kneeling figure."

When we pray, we see God work. At this critical and turbulent time in our nation's history, we do not need more of what man can accomplish. We need God to do what only He can do, and that will only come if we seek Him through prayer.

In this passage, we are first told what **types** of prayer to pray. Paul used a number of specific words, and each of these has significance. The first is *"supplications,"* which is the most earnest type of prayers—specific, fervent, and concentrated. We need more than simply praying over meals, before bedtime, and at the start of a church service. We must have designated seasons set aside to seek the Lord's face.

When was the last time you made supplication instead of simply saying a prayer? Now is the time to begin to concentrate our prayers on specific needs. The Bible says in James 5:16, *"The effectual fervent prayer of a righteous man availeth much."* In the next verse, we are given an illustration of this truth from the life of Elijah. It simply says, *"he prayed earnestly."* Literally, in his praying—he actually prayed! I wonder how many of our prayers have true prayer in them?

Remember that when Israel had her worst king, King Ahab, she had her greatest prophet. Elijah was not great because of his abilities. He was used because of his nearness to God. The key to the nation is not who is seated at the seat of government, but who is kneeling at the throne of God! In the worst days, God does His best work. Ask Him.

The second word in 2 Timothy 2:1 is *"prayers."* That is the more general term we often use, but it is meant to encompass our entire life. Remember that we are instructed in 1 Thessalonians 5:17, *"Pray without ceasing."* We are to pray all throughout the day. There are definite seasons of prayer, and then there is prayer that permeates every part of life. Charles Spurgeon said, "The habit of prayer is good but the spirit of prayer is better."

The next term, *"intercessions,"* refers to the highest level of prayer. This was Christ's pattern of prayer when He was on earth. Listen to His prayer in John 17, and look at the intensity of His prayer in the Garden of Gethsemane (Hebrews 5:7)! This is the type of prayer in which Jesus is engaged for us at this very moment. According to Romans 8:34, He is seated *"even at the right hand of God, who also maketh intercession for us."* Jesus is praying for you today. Praise God for this truth!

For whom are you making intercession? When we begin to intercede for others and bear one another's burdens, we are entering into the Lord's work with Him, agreeing with Christ in prayer for others. *"Bear ye one another's burdens, and so fulfil the law of Christ"* (Galatians 6:2).

The temptation in these perilous times is to get very self-centered, and pray only for ourselves and those we know and love. But we must not stop there. Intercessory prayer can influence people you may never personally meet. Remember that your prayers can go where you cannot!

The last type of prayer mentioned in verse 1 is *"giving of thanks."* Thanksgiving is the key that opens the door to prayer. Psalm 100:4 instructs us, *"Enter into his gates with thanksgiving, and into his courts with praise."* According to Philippians 4:6, *"In every thing by prayer and supplication with thanksgiving let your requests be made known unto God."* Begin and end with thanksgiving.

While you are asking God today for big things, don't forget to praise Him for what He has already done, what He is doing now, and what He will do in the future in answer to your prayer of faith. Thanksgiving will increase your faith.

We are also told in this passage **for whom to pray**. The first group is mentioned at the end of verse 1: *"for all men."* You cannot pray for the wrong person! We should be praying for everyone to come to know the Lord Jesus Christ as Savior. At the heart of these prayer principles is the fact that God desires for *"all men to be saved, and to come unto the knowledge of the truth"* (verse 4). You can always know that you are praying in the will of God when you are praying for any person to come to know Him in a personal way (2 Peter 3:9). Do you have a prayer list of souls? If we want to reach an entire nation, it is accomplished one soul at a time.

The beginning of verse 2 mentions that we are to pray for *"kings, and all that are in authority."* In our country, we have a president, a vice president, senators, representatives, governors, mayors, and other elected officials. Each of these individuals need our prayers. Regardless of political affiliations and opinions, we should pray that God will guide them, protect them, and give them wisdom. We have no right to lift our voice in criticism against leaders if we have neglected to lift our voice, first, in prayer on their behalf. Before lodging a complaint against an elected official, offer your complaint in prayer to God. He can accomplish much more through your prayer than you can through your complaint alone.

Three reasons are given in verses 2-3 to show us **why we pray**. First, we pray because it is good for us. We pray so *"that we may lead a quiet and peaceable life in all godliness and honesty."* With the amount of division and fighting that has become the norm in modern life, the *"quiet and peaceable life"* sounds very attractive. This life is only a result of prayer. Through our prayer for others, God will work in us. Remember that God turned the captivity of Job when he prayed for his friends (Job 42:10).

When the children of Israel were taken captive by an idolatrous people God even instructed them to pray for their captors. Jeremiah 29:7 says, *"And seek the peace of the city whither I have caused you to be carried away captives, and pray unto the Lord for it: for in the peace thereof shall ye have peace."* As we pray, God works on both ends.

Intercessory prayer is also good for others, as noted by the earlier mention of God's desire to see people saved. The kindest thing you can do for those you love is to pray for them! And, Jesus taught that we should not only pray for our friends, but for our enemies (Matthew 5:43-45).

Ultimately, the greatest reason we pray is for the glory of God. The purest motive for prayer should not be our comfort or someone else's need, it should be God's glory: *"For this is good and acceptable in the sight of God our Saviour."*

When Jesus taught His disciples to pray, He started with, *"Our Father which art in heaven, Hallowed be thy name. Thy kingdom come, Thy will be done in earth, as it is in heaven"* (Matthew 6:9-10). Let your prayers begin with God and lead to God, for then you will truly know how to pray in a way that honors Him.

Finally, Paul also instructs us **how to pray**. *"I will therefore that men pray every where, lifting up holy hands, without wrath and doubting"* (verse 8). While you cannot pray in the wrong place, you can pray in the wrong way. We are to lift up *"holy hands."* It is essential that our heart and our hands are clean by removing all sin from our lives (Psalm 24:3-4; James 4:8). *"If I regard iniquity in my heart, the Lord will not hear me"* (Psalms

66:18). When we have dealt with sin in our life, we have opened the lines of communication to our Heavenly Father.

The great need of our nation is a mighty move of God, and our first priority is prayer. When our personal priorities become the priorities God desires for us to have, then we will begin to see Him at work, not only in our lives, but also in our nation. First things first.

· 2 PETER 2:5-9 ·
NOAH AND LOT

If you are the right kind of Christian, you will be the right kind of citizen. All Christians have a dual citizenship. We are temporary, earthly citizens of the nation where God has providentially allowed us to live and we are eternal, heavenly citizens of a much better country! In the words of the gospel song, "This world is not my home, I'm just passing through." The Lord's people ought to be the most caring, principled, and helpful citizens of their present nation, but they must also remember that they are only pilgrims on their way home (Hebrews 11:13-16).

God's people should be informed and engaged. We should vote righteously and participate in the process. But what eternal impact can a believer make for the country in which he or she lives? To answer that, let's examine an Old Testament story found in a New Testament passage.

The Bible says in 2 Peter 2:5-9:

> *And spared not the old world, but saved Noah the eighth person, a preacher of righteousness, bringing in the flood upon the world of the ungodly; And turning the cities of Sodom and Gomorrha into ashes condemned them with an overthrow, making them an ensample unto those that after should live ungodly; And delivered just Lot, vexed with the filthy conversation of the wicked: (For that righteous man dwelling among them, in seeing and hearing, vexed his righteous soul from day to day with their unlawful deeds;) The Lord knoweth how to deliver the godly out of temptations, and to reserve the unjust unto the day of judgment to be punished.*

It is unique to see how God links the experiences of Noah and Lot throughout Scripture. These men, both introduced in the book of Genesis, are well-known Bible characters. One is famous and one is infamous, but God uses them as positive and negative examples. Though separated by 400 years of history, as well as a considerable amount of geography, they are given as illustrations in this passage in 2 Peter. Jesus also referred to them both in Luke 17 when talking about the time just before He returns.

THE NEED OF OUR NATION

Why does the Bible connect the stories of Noah and Lot? What is the Lord teaching us?

There is a comparison, as both men lived in evil days just like we do today. There is also a contrast in that Noah spoke the truth while Lot was silent. Which one are you? Do you speak up for righteousness, or do you prefer not to "rock the boat" and to stay behind the scenes?

Each of us is either a Noah or a Lot. Through both of these men, God is reminding us that we are responsible for the world in which we live. While we cannot control how others respond, we will give an account for how we represent the Lord in our nation and in our generation. Noah was accountable for the testimony he gave in his day. So was Lot. The same is true for us in our day.

Noah is identified as *"a preacher of righteousness"*—he did more than build a boat! Sadly, there is no record that Lot ever opened his mouth to speak truth to a wicked culture. Lot was delivered by God's grace because the Lord always delivers His own, but he did not show others how they could be delivered.

Most of us do not get to choose where we live. None of us can choose when we live. What we can choose, however, is how we are going to live in this place and time.

Lot made a bad decision. His tragic story is found in Genesis 19. Although it is a negative story, there are tremendous, positive truths for us to apply as we live today.

Lot's great failure was not so much in what he did as in what he did not do. Is there anything that the Lord has prompted you to do that you have not yet done? We are told in James 4:17, *"Therefore to him that knoweth to do good, and doeth it not, to him it is sin."*

We know Lot was a believer because the Bible refers to him as a *"just"* man and a *"righteous man."* It is a reminder that while you may know Jesus as your Savior, you should consider what you are doing to bring others to a saving knowledge of Him. He also had a wonderful heritage. His uncle Abraham had taught him a great deal while exemplifying a life of faith. We too have a great heritage, but the issue for us is not what we have been given but what we will leave behind when we are gone. What are we doing with what we have been given?

Like every man, Lot had a conscience, because the Scriptures say he was *"vexed"* by what went on around him. It is one thing to hate the darkness around you; it is quite another thing to pierce it with light. Many Christians are bothered by the wickedness in our nation, but we must be participants and not spectators in this spiritual battle.

The Scriptures seem to suggest that Lot was even a kind and gracious man. We see this in the hospitality shown to the two strangers who came to his door just before Sodom and Gomorrah fell, and how he tried to protect them. Yet the sad fact remains that Lot did not make a difference in Sodom.

God's people are left in this world to make a difference. Sodom was not saved because there was no salt and light there. In the words of Jesus in Matthew 5:13-16:

> *Ye are the salt of the earth: but if the salt have lost his savour, wherewith shall it be salted? it is thenceforth good for nothing, but to be cast out, and to be trodden under foot of men. Ye are the light of the world. A city that is set on an hill cannot be hid. Neither do men light a candle, and put it under a bushel, but on a candlestick; and it giveth light unto all that are in the house. Let your light so shine before men, that they may see your good works, and glorify your Father which is in heaven.*

If Lot had simply done what a follower of God should do, according to what Jesus said in Matthew 11 and Luke 17, Sodom would have remained! Let us consider what Lot did not do that we must do.

Lot did not use his influence for God.

He had influence; everyone does. In Genesis 19, when the angels arrived at Sodom, Lot was sitting at the gate. It was a place of authority, where the political leaders sat. This was a man who had influence, but refused to use it for God.

As believers, our own influence is a powerful weapon for advancing the gospel. Within your own circle of influence, are you making an impact for Christ and His kingdom? Have those closest to you seen the difference that Jesus Christ has made in your life? God gives influence, but we must use it.

What are you doing with the influence God has given you? You might think your influence is small, but you should use what you have. There is a ripple effect: as we are obedient, God gives us more influence.

We live in a world where people are constantly trying to build a larger platform. We should begin by using the influence we already have. Start where you are to influence others for good and for God. Share the gospel of Jesus Christ and point as many people as possible to Him.

Lot did not instruct his family.

Lot's greatest failure was in his own home; that is where influence must begin. The quickest way to lose a nation is to lose the family. The battle in our nation is not won in the houses of government; it is won in our homes.

No one is a better Christian than the Christian they are in the privacy of their own home. Spiritual awakenings do not begin in the houses of government; they begin in our house and the church house. *"For the time is come that judgment must begin at the house of God…"* (1 Peter 4:17). God always begins with His own people.

Lot's sons-in-law mocked his faith, and his daughters were corrupted long before he offered them up to the mob outside his house. Before their gross immorality with their father on the mountain outside Sodom, their consciences had already been defiled.

Not only did he lose his children, but his wife sadly turned back toward Sodom and was turned into a pillar of salt. She became physically the very thing she and her husband refused to be spiritually! That is why Jesus said in Luke 17:32, *"Remember Lot's wife."* She was more in love with her life than with her Lord. We must not fail to instruct our families in the things of God.

Lot did not intercede for others.

There is no record of Lot ever building an altar. In contrast, everywhere his uncle Abraham went, he built an altar. In fact, he even prayed for Sodom (Genesis 18:16-33). But he did so from outside the city. No one inside the city was praying.

Remember that in many ways Lot is contrasted with Noah. When Noah got off the ark, the first thing he did was build an altar (Genesis 8:20). Lot, however, was more concerned with building a reputation and building a life, than he was building an altar.

God is always looking for intercessors. In Isaiah 59:16 we read, *"And he saw that there was no man, and wondered that there was no intercessor: therefore his arm brought salvation unto him; and his righteousness, it sustained him."* Christ became the mediator, the go-between, the ultimate intercessor for sinners (Isaiah 53:12; 1 Timothy 2:5). God's heart is always to reconcile sinners to Himself and yet so few of His people have this heart to see others turned to the Lord.

The only two times we have recorded that God wondered or marveled was because of unbelief (Mark 6:6) and because of prayerlessness (Isaiah 59:16). A lack of faith and a lack of prayer are still the great problems in our world. Where are the intercessors?

Samuel Chadwick wrote, "Satan dreads nothing but prayer. His one concern is to keep saints from praying. He fears nothing from prayerless studies, prayerless work, prayerless religion. He laughs at our toil. He mocks at our wisdom. But he trembles when we pray."

The great man of prayer, E.M. Bounds said, "Prayer breaks all bars, dissolves all chains, opens all prisons, and widens all straits by which God's saints have been held." We must not miss the divine opportunity and personal responsibility that are given to us in prayer.

One of the saddest verses in Scripture is Ezekiel 22:30, where God cries, *"And I sought for a man among them, that should make up the hedge, and stand in the gap before me for the land, that I should not destroy it: but I found none."* Moses stood in the gap (Psalm 106:23; Exodus 32:31-32). Phinehas stood in the gap (Psalm 106:30; Numbers 25:7-8). Aaron stood in the gap (Numbers 16:48). Esther stood in the gap (Esther 4:16). Paul stood in the gap (Romans 9:1-3, 10:1). Who will stand in the gap for your city, state, and nation?

Jeremiah wept over Jerusalem in the Old Testament (Jeremiah 9:1), and Jesus wept over the same city in the New Testament (Luke 19:41). In every age, someone must take up the burden and seek the salvation of the lost. This is something every Christian can do.

Each one of us can use our influence, teach our families, and intercede for souls. Jesus is coming soon. I want to be Noah, not Lot. May God help us make our lives count for Him while we can. We are only seasonal settlers here. Be the best Christian citizen you can be and tell everyone about the better country to come.

· CONCLUSION ·
IT'S YOUR TURN

The person most interested in the spiritual welfare of a nation, and most concerned with that country's direction, ought to be those who love God and want truth and righteousness for their children. If anyone should be on their knees praying for their nation right now, it is those who say that they know and love the Lord.

If our country has so many churches, believers and preachers, why are we making so little impact? We have learned to organize, strategize, sensationalize, philosophize, commercialize, and sermonize, but we have forgotten how to agonize!

THE NEED OF OUR NATION

Samuel Chadwick summarized it well: "Nothing would turn the nation back to God so surely and so quickly as a church that prayed and prevailed. The world will never believe in a religion in which there is no supernatural power. A rationalized faith, a socialized church, and a moralized gospel may gain applause, but they awaken no conviction and win no converts."

We must pray for our own nation and ask God to do what only He can do. As we begin to pray, we will see God at work. Prayer is the greatest work because when we pray, we see the hand of Heaven move on Earth. We want God's blessing, but we need brokenness (James 4:8-10). Revivals always begin in humbled hearts.

Many men and women of prayer have served the Lord and their nation in previous generations. It's your turn. Will you accept this challenge now to start praying for your country, as one part of a unified prayer team bombarding Heaven on its behalf? Would you prioritize your life so that you can keep this divine appointment with a holy God each day?

Pray for our land, for its leaders, and for the Lord to do something great at this critical hour in history. It is prayer time in our country. If you love the Lord and our land, begin praying definite prayers in faith today. This is the need of our nation.

GEORGE WASHINGTON'S PRAYER

Our nation's first president understood the necessity of prayer in his own life. One of the most vivid images of George Washington is the famous painting of him kneeling in the snow at Valley Forge in 1777. However, it is important to know that Washington did not begin by praying for his nation, he lived as a man of prayer daily. The following is taken from George Washington's prayer journal and reveals a heart that is both humble before God and hungry for spiritual help:

> O eternal and everlasting God, I presume to present myself this morning before thy Divine majesty, beseeching thee to accept of my humble and hearty thanks, that it hath pleased thy great goodness to keep and preserve me the night past from all the dangers poor mortals are subject to, and has given me sweet and pleasant sleep, whereby I find my body refreshed and comforted for performing the duties of this day, in which I beseech thee to defend me from all perils of body and soul.

> Direct my thoughts, words and work. Wash away my sins in the immaculate blood of the lamb, and

purge my heart by thy Holy Spirit, from the dross
of my natural corruption, that I may with more
freedom of mind and liberty of will serve thee, the
everlasting God, in righteousness and holiness this
day, and all the days of my life.

Increase my faith in the sweet promises of the
Gospel. Give me repentance from dead works.
Pardon my wanderings, and direct my thoughts
unto thyself, the God of my salvation. Teach me
how to live in thy fear, labor in thy service, and
ever to run in the ways of thy commandments.
Make me always watchful over my heart, that
neither the terrors of conscience, the loathing of
holy duties, the love of sin, nor an unwillingness
to depart this life, may cast me into a spiritual
slumber. But daily frame me more and more into
the likeness of thy Son Jesus Christ, that living
in thy fear, and dying in thy favor, I may in thy
appointed time attain the resurrection of the just
unto eternal life. Bless my family, friends and
kindred, unite us all in praising and glorifying
thee in all our works begun, continued, and ended,
when we shall come to make our last account
before thee blessed Saviour, who hath taught us
thus to pray, our Father.

When young Washington first left home, his mother gave
him this advice: "Remember that God is our only one trust.

To Him, I commend you…My son, neglect not the duty of secret prayer."

If we want to see divine intervention, we must give ourselves to private intercession. *"But thou, when thou prayest, enter into thy closet, and when thou hast shut thy door, pray to thy Father which is in secret; and thy Father which seeth in secret shall reward thee openly"* (Matthew 6:6). The secret to open blessing is secret prayer. From a quiet place you can touch Heaven and God can touch the world. *"Lord, teach us to pray"* (Luke 11:1).

Following God's Word & Finding Christ's Joy.

Walk with us through God's Word and discover
the joy of journeying with Jesus each day at:

enjoyingthejourney.org

Daily broadcast · Helpful Resources · Online Bible Studies